From the Cauldron

THE HIPPOCAMPUS PRESS POETRY LIBRARY

Eyes of the God: The Weird Fiction and Poetry of R. H. Barlow (2002)
Clark Ashton Smith, *The Last Oblivion: Best Fantastic Poems* (2003)
George Sterling, *The Thirst of Satan: Poems of Fantasy and Terror* (2003)
R. Nemo Hill, *The Strange Music of Erich Zann* (2004)
Out of the Immortal Night: Selected Works of Samuel Loveman (2004)
Sanctity and Sin: The Collected Poems and Prose Poems of Donald Wandrei (2007)
Clark Ashton Smith, *The Complete Poetry and Translations* (2007–08; 3 vols.)
Clark Ashton Smith, *The Hashish-Eater* (2008)
Donald Sidney-Fryer, *The Atlantis Fragments: The Trilogy of Songs and Sonnets Atlantean* (2008)
Nora May French, *The Outer Gate: The Collected Poems* (2009)

From the Cauldron

Fred Phillips

Hippocampus Press

New York

Published by Hippocampus Press
P.O. Box 641, New York, NY 10156.
http://www.hippocampuspress.com

Cover illustration by Howard Wandrei
Cover design by Barbara Briggs Silbert.
Hippocampus Press logo designed by Anastasia Damianakos.

First Edition
1 3 5 7 9 8 6 4 2

ISBN 978-0-9844802-6-5

To Dorothea Nissen Phillips—ne plus ultra

Contents

The Fair Folk

The Fair Folk

There was a time when once the Earth we walked
Knew sun, the kiss of rain, the sting of snow
And hiding, heard the yeomen as they talked
Of earthly things we were not meant to know.
And in our fathers' time, when bosk and byre
Each thatched roof's weathered dovecote cooed and purred;
Near shadowed wood a crone would lay her fire,
Who cackled o'er her cauldron as she stirred,
And whither flown those ancient, vanished years
When night to our abode strange pilgrims sent
By lanthorn-light, long ere the dawn appeared
And none knew whence they came, or where they went . . .
'Tis main hard, even when you know yourself,
To be a creature known to men as Elf.

Metamorphosis

The northern Queen the potent chalice fills
With fearful scream, and dark of deadly night;
The rosy hue of wind-kist colour chills
The dread potation, whence there is no flight.
Her gloomy mirror's face the Grecian masque
Unto her questing heart, in icy tones,
Responds to secret queries that she asks,
Whilst pale, green light falls on her chamber's stones.
Outside, the tempest howls, as though the wind,
Despited yet, for all his Titan's breath,
Is forced his quarry's peril to rescind
To Time, that aged harbinger of Death;
Yet meanwhile, in the forest, blithe and gay,
The little men their ancient ballads play. . . .

Giliniel

That rose hath never faded from her face
Like pale blooms that she prest between the leaves—
Fortune's handmaid, blest with every grace
That Time and Nature, twixt the twain, conceives.
Who, save wight from beyond the fields we know,
May 'scape enrapturement beneath her hands?
Above whose tread the moon doth brighter glow,
The unicorn obeys her least command.
The dew calls 'sister' whom the wind adores,
A banquet for the famished eye, in sooth;
The mistress of a myriad of lores
Which ardently enhance the search for truth.
To love her, well we ken the world were lost—
But love we must—and that at any cost!

Sleep

The babe dreams peacefully within its crib;
The King within the stony mountain sleeps;
The penman nods above his ebon nib,
Whilst rosy-fingered dawn upon them creeps.
In bliss the slave his aching bones repose;
His master, lapped in silence, softly snores;
Fatigue doth gently aching eyelids close
As warders doze before the great bronze doors.
Grey tendrils curl out from the dragon's nares;
The wee folk slumber ere their derring-day;
No sound is heard upon the creaking stairs,
For Nature hath her noises laid away.
There be but one whom Sleep as yet defies—
And he hath been cast down from Paradise!

De la Marche

No loup-garou, mayhap, but certes he
Were rather more a spirit than a man
That we and our age evoked, to be
O'er chasms of oblivion, the span.
Now they have quoted him, who scarce recall
The darkness of the years before he came,
When many prayed a man like him to fall
Upon our lists and make them clean again.
Of entsaumple full gentle e'er hath been
Our ghostly ally, seldom in our soil,
Had we a world to roam, or war to win.
Without his counsel, vain were all our toil,
But be thou ghost or no, if this verse scan,
I'll own my debt to gentle Count Jehan!

One More

"But one more blow," the rearguard called and fell,
The pass behind him cluttered with the dead;
"But one more bite," the glutton knows too well
The path down which his arrant vice hath led.
"But one more song," reluctant students yield
Their nights of foamy pleasure to the dawn;
"But one more bout"—and up the battered shield
Is lifted o'er the jackboot-trampled lawn.
"But one more glass"—the toper greets his rue,
Fatigued with semi-insensated mind,
"But one more verse"—asprawl upon the dew,
Aurora's watch leaves Nyx's cloak behind.
And if my love would grant me perfect bliss,
Then I beseech of her but one more kiss!

The Little Stone

As I sat 'neath a leafy bough one summer afternoon,
The sun in radiant glory setting, waiting for the moon,
I stared in contemplation at a weathered little stone
That lay amid the verdant grasses, quiet and alone.
"And whither art thy brethren?" I asked the little mite,
As Helios drew across his face the purple veil of night;
"My brethren guard the valleys of a hundred mighty streams;
We line the roads from Arcady to Ossian's land of dreams;
'Mid verdure lush at twilight's hush, in forest, field, and brook,
With trailing ivy creepers to illuminate each nook."
With measured satisfaction the stony fragment spake
Whilst roundabout the birds had stilled their piping in the brake.
"The tomb of Baba Khan is carved with floral arabesque
That Feizal cut with angel's touch at Savatla's behest;
The statues of the heroes from Varangia to Khand
Are carven from my brethren through the realms of Frankistan;
The Royal Ones sleep peacefully beneath their painted tombs,
Bedecked with gold and faience in their painted treasure-rooms.
The Dorian hath his granite, the Roman porphyry;
(The Huns sleep on the rocky scarp of distant Tartary)
The early Picts their circled stones on Wiltshire's meadows raised
That they who followed after might behold and be amazed,
And when they finally lay to rest the great Chief of the North,

His cairn will keep him doon so he wull no' gae bounding forth."
"O, thanks to thee, thou little stone," I quoth, "my thanks to thee;
With what, I prithee, will they carve the stone that covers me?"
"O friend," replied the little stone, "I surely am no seer
That my rede should foretell what men will 'scribe upon thy bier;
But fill thy life with good works, and with greed and pride be done,
And thou need never fear what Time will write upon thy stone."

Fleeting Hours

The ruby splendour of the setting sun
That decks the Heavens with a holy light;
The herald of the time when day is done
Before the rising of the Queen of Night;
The twitter of the birds at dawn of day
In deepest forest known by beasts alone,
As breezes make the leafy branches sway
And with thy leman, make the sweetest moan;
The cauldron's odour in the autumn's haze
With mutton, sage, and onion richly pent
That none forget until their final days
These earthly splendours, straight from Heaven sent—
O Name whose glory all Creation sings:
Wherefore dost Thou take from us these things?

Frederick of Holland

He came from the land where the warriors stand
        And the women stand at their side;
He hath roused from its sleep in the vasty deep
        The heart of our nation's pride.
And his sign we ken, for we honour them
        Who have quit the fields we know;
With his arms he bore much eldritch lore—
        May his road be long to go.
We had sought their spoor on the lonely moor,
        Where the anchorite breaks his bread;
We had followed them back from the winding track
        Past the barrows of the dead.
We had combed this hills and had dragged the rills
        For a sign of the silver horn,
Yet we failed to ken (being mortal men)
        The ways of the Unicorn.

On the Heath

My mother taught me weirdings at her knee beside the hearth,
To love the untamed creatures of the sky, the sea, and earth;
Not to slay them needlessly but learn the songs they sing,
That they might tell me privily of what the future brings.

And it may be that one day none will celebrate our rites—
Our wands and athames gather dust and never see the light;
But while the fire's crackling, let us set about our toil—
Stoke the fire, sisters, and let the cauldron boil!

Madrigal to Dian Alene

No quare in keep e'er kept so deep
As I keep long from thee,
For day and night thy vision bright
Must linger, haunting me;
No day hath pass'd that of my glass
Do not thy health partake;
Were it not wrong that for so long
Must my sad heart still ache?

I cannot spy the sun or sky,
The green earth hides its view;
For so long thou hast strain'd my vow
That I have sworn to you;
Thine absence drowns my joy in sounds
I'd never make to thee;
The sun may rise o'er azure skies,
But nevermore on me.

A Winter Night's Sleep

Late came I, to the halls of men,
Briefly stayed, then forth again;
With many a tale served I at meat,
Warming hearts better than Juul-log's heat.
Mead quickens blood, but my tales start
Ever and ever inside the heart.
Heidrek himself did not disdain
To hear my lays in language plain;
Hear me now, as I recite
What befell me one winter's night.

The snows were heavy, the forest deep
As I fared forth to find a keep
The homeliest hovel wherein to sleep.
So cold like Fimbulvetr came
The snows like swords, o'er hill and plain;
My breath like cloudy vapours swirled
In icy tendrils 'round me curled,
My hands and feet felt cold as stone
In Boreas' grip, chilled to the bone.
I thought I would draw my last breath
And be denied a Viking's death
I sank in drifts upon my knees.
When suddenly, beyond the trees

A golden glimmer pierced the gloom
And saved me from a frozen doom.
I stumbled forward, and I saw
Nestled in a piney draw
A humble hut, its window bright
With one single, solitary light.
"Odin!" I breathed, smote at the portal,
"Ope unto me, a frozen mortal,
A night's lodging of thee, I pray,
At dawn's light I'll be on my way."
The door swung open; such was my fate,
A small fire glowered on the grate,
A table rude, some stools to match
And tablecloth with neat-sewn patch.
My host, a tall and grizzled man,
Beckoned me in, and then began
To gather bread and meat and mead,
And to my tale to pay good heed.
"A night's lodging thou wilt share,
Since thou'rt so fearless as to dare
To lodge with the Daudrherran so."
"Better with thee than in the snow,"
I replied. "I charge a toll,"

He said; "Art thou so bold
As would 'neath one roof draw thy breath
In fellowship with the Lord of Death?"
"Now thou," quoth I, "art very old,
And therefore some ken ye must hold
Of hospitality's ancient laws—"
The Daudrherran turned and paused,
And quoth, "Aye, these wot I full well,
But mine own law do I compel
Each living creature to obey
Gin they lodge here or far away.
Thy life, I would ye understand,
I hold now hither in my hand.
Now thou must make a solemn oath
To be my man and serve in sooth
Until I send at last for thee
To walk my unknown paths with me."
Thus swore I well. His hand was cold.
The oath was, certes, very old:
"I am thy man against the world,"
And then before the fire I curled
On furs, my ragged mantle drew
To shield me from the morning dew.

When I awoke, a fire was lain,
And on the table, fare full plain;
Warm ale sat in its stony pot
(At least the pease-porridge was hot).
I wondered if I had but dreamed
Of the Daudrherran? So it seemed;
Fared forth again, and found my way
To where men's habitations lay.
Some men are skeptics; without fail
They look askance when I tell my tale;
Others sit agape and drink
My words as parchment swallows ink.
But none of them have ever dared
To travel whither I have fared.
'Tis wisely writ: good meat, good bread,
A tale or two, and then to bed.
Be careful where you lay your head.

The Old Tavern

The horses' hoofs strike fiery sparks from off the cobbled street
Of Sherrick-town where Roman road and Saxon ox-trail meet;
The Captain is a sturdy carle; grim-visaged, darkened scowl;
A broadsword for his rosary, a chain-coif for his cowl.

They clatter into the courtyard of the ancient Druid's Head,
The weeds that from the paving sprout have long ago been dead.
The Captain with his pommel raps on the weathered door,
"Open in the King's name"—all is quiet as before.

The horses shuffle, snort, and start; the air with evil fraught;
The men-at-arms are wondering if their errand is for naught.
Again the Captain bangs and cries, "Now open for the Crown!
Surrender up the Red Fitzhugh or I'll tear your tavern down!"

Inside the darkness echoes still; the shadows sunk in gloom;
The cloak of Time is yet unmoved for puny mortal doom;
And for the third time raps the hilt upon the weathered planks—
"I've a warrant for Fitzhugh; now ye may earn thy sovereign's
thanks!"

A tiny crack of light peeps from behind the ancient door
As it slowly swings wide open, lamplight streaming on the floor,
And a little girl with flaxen hair, besmirched with tear-streaked face,
Pipes up, "My daddy's gone—now get ye hence from off this place!"

A flash of memory smites the grizzled Captain's iron heart,
And then a voice behind him speaks, "Per'aps we should depart,
Beggin' your pardon, sur—" The Captain lifts his horse's reins,
"A seemly tale the King to tell—we've nothing for our pains!"

And turns his steed about; the horsemen follow, two by two,
The child stands still and watches with her shining eyes of blue
Till the echoes of the hoofbeats melt into the misty night
And the tavern door shuts out once more the flickering
candlelight. . . .

Ode to Asbjorn Gustavsson Haarfagr

Now is a fire kindled in the north
That puts to shame the gleam of Bifrost;
The young Squire, pride of the Parsus prince,
Fair of locks and brave of heart,
Hath wrested the Laurel Throne of Oster-rike
From its wonted champions, Fire and Ice,
And maketh reign in the East of so goodly comport
That Travelers fare from far veldts
To win honour in his Royal lists.
Soft of speech, with brand like adder's tongue,
This were a good ring-giver; this King
Despiseth not the rede of old, but gives place
In the fyrd to the worthy! Let speech be made to him
Full gently; Hugi and Hemi spread their pinions
At his Father's side, and battle-worthy thegns
Have been brought low before him;
This is our true King . . .

Final Quest

We lost Arnaud when we passed Devil's Peak
Amid a horde of incandescent Trolls;
Of Erik it were better not to speak,
Unhorsed as he was at the Well of Souls;
How mourned the scarlet sky when Cormac fell—
A Captain whom the Bards will ever praise;
Of Ivor I will sing his song to Hell
And bear his loss until the End of Days.
How Fate has thinned our host the blind can see,
For few are we who rode upon our quest,
And now on winded steeds sit you and me,
And wonder whom Pale Death will winnow next.
Into my scabbard my notched blade I slide,
For this Road is the last that we shall ride.

Bane of Aeacus

Through a darkling labyrinth of vines
That transfigures a long-accustomed place
To day where Apollyon reclines
And renders inexplicable its face,
Whence from tenebrous depth a ruby glare
Of Things averse to every Adam's son
Bide lurking near a downward-turning stair
To guerdon for the deeds that every one
Hath in unheeding lifetime truly wrought,
Monitored by Shadows from Beyond
Who from their deeds the Seal of Judgment bought
And exiled to where none are ever found,
Their deeds by any means to expiate
That by the ruthless glass were rendered late.

The Gathering of Clan Creachain

The dew on the heather, like sparkling pearls,
Greets morn in the Highlands 'mid echoing skirls
And the sun o'er MacGlomach beams fairly again
On the points of the pikes in Earl Aonghais' train.

O, weep not, my Mary, for fain would I go
To serve the braw lairdie and smite at his foe;
For never before hath fair Scotia known
Sae fearless a champion of hearth, hill, and home.

The Sassenach soldiers ha' nailed to the oak
A reward for his capture—they'll na hae their joke!
In fen, brae, and marsh we will harry their host;
Their hopes to chain Scotia will sairly be lost.

We're a pruit folk, my darlin', and never for long
Ha' our foemen had vic'try to rime in their songs;
We sheltered the bonny Earl under our roof—
'Neath his shield take we shelter; our service be proof.

O gie me that while on my deathbed I lie
To aim one fair shaft into Scotia's sky;
The twang of the bow is the Iarl's fond refrain—
May his heirs hear sich music from Creachain again!

I see them a-marching, my Mary, sae brave
They tramp by the cataract near Fingal's cave
Wi' bonnets and plumes held aloft in the wind;
Ye'll search far an' wide to find men of their kind.

Their claymores have ne'er tasted honest Scots blood,
Their foemen ha' grappled and died where they stood;
I see all the brave Clans wi' their banners unfurled—
O when ha' sic men e'er drawn breath in the world?

O keep a' thy baubles, they medals and such—
In the Lowlands they're bonny, but in battle not much;
Just gie uns oat-porridge an' a stoup of sma' ale,
An' we'll wreath him in vic'try, or die if we fail!

O, ye shud ha' been there, when the red sun went doon,
An' the men o' the camp by the fire stood round;
Ere we put the first morsel o' food to our lips,
We made service to Aonghais wi' his hands on his hips.

Then fa' to, my brawnies, and fear noght the nicht,
Tomorrow the sun will shine, airly and bricht
An' on mony a foeman will never again—
Who ha' come to do battle with Aonghais' men.

Ere I lay on my helm to sleep, wi' my brand nigh
I heard a young laddie, wi' tears in his eye,
Pray, "O Laird, 'tis nowt dying I fear, or the pain,
But ye maun keep Laird Aonghais, lest he should be slain."

An' I thoght, "Noo mony guid Scotsmen an'a
Were a-praying that night he be spared from a fa
An' I thoght, "Noo sairly the Laird won't deny
That his people do love him, like birds love the sky."

For he's hame in the Highlands, where his roots have fang spread
An' neath honest folks' roofs may the Iarl make his bed
Who wish him fair weal, may they prosper in peace—
An' whoso wish him else—God ha' mercy on these!

The Formula

Not Pilgrim Grey nor Arthur's Ward
Than Shadow deeper than the night
Bore vigour greater than the sword
When finally the stars were right.
No keeper of forbidden scrolls
Primeval parchment limned with keys
That lay in wait for careless souls
Who headlong ran afoul of these.
A chaos from an unknown source
Enveloped them who dared recite
The formula that loosed its force
And shrouded them with deathless night.
Heed well these caveats, O friend,
And keep from such a gruesome end.

The Tale of the Scribe

Dedicated with profoundest respect and esteem to Duke Cariadoc of the Bow and to All Those Who Serve the Muse

O Duke, thou foremost of the age,
Be pleased to read upon this page
What I, thy servant, have inscrib'd
The love of Lore to keep alive.
My labours are but humble script:
The centuries may hide my crypt
In dark, complete obscurity
Whilst Fame forever blesses thee;
But lest ye hold me ill-content,
To thee, my whole heart, all unpent
Will straight confess felicity
That Allah hath so smiled on me.
Let all the nations praise His Name:
To give His chosen servants fame,
And armed us with the pot and quill
That humble scribes may wreak His will.
No alabaster walls may hold
Their treasures wrought in rarest gold,
Nor any works by man's hand wrought

Shall sweeter taste than fruits of thought.
The Sidi Jehan doth engage
With proven minstrels of the age
To rear a haven in the East,
Where bards may elevate our feast;
But never think, O noblest Duke,
That my conscience would not rebuke
My every moment of the day,
Flew I not with this rede straightway
Unto thy gates with deep salute
Upon this question— ('twere not moot!)
A BARDIC COLLEGE will arise;
If rede of this doth thee surprise,
Ten thousand thousand pardons crave . . .
But thou, whose every work were brave,
From hewing infidels to their doom
(An they give thee scant elbow-room)
To wine and kumiss to imbibe
As with great thanks thy humble scribe
Thy littlest deed makes great deeds small,
And justly sung without our hall.
And thus we pray, come thou this year

To read thy works; mayhap to hear
The offerings of other folk
In whose warm hearts thou hast awoke
With good works and civility,
Abiding love for poesy.

Burleycon 1973

If I had done the pleasure of a King
That liked him well enough to grant me boon,
And His Grace said, "Choose thou anything
Within our Royal gift beneath the Moon,
And it were thine—" Then I would say, "My lord,
A kindled hearth; a row of tankards full;
With every viand spread, a groaning board,
And finally, sweet Thalia's joys to cull,
My comrades, blithe with song and merry jest—
And crowning all, that dismal hours be check'd,
Our own dear Orphic Jason"—such request
Of all rare treasures, chiefest in respect
We honour thus ourselves, to voice abroad
His praises to a most munificent God.

Chanson de Guerre

Sling, stone; whirr forth; smite the crenelled wall;
Forth, ye minions; up the banner; onwards, captains tall;
Bend bow, heft flamberge, smite, ye laggards, smite!
Pull down the stones about their ears—we dine in Vosges tonight!

Tramp, steed, bear forth men to saddle born;
Jingle, harness, roll drum, wind the ancient horn;
We will show them who know soldiers from a crow;
As they burn, they will learn what we already know!

Range spears, plant stakes, archer, stand by bow,
Their front file is a scant mile, you must bring them low!
God who to our fathers gave victory in war,
Help us to fight, Lord, as men have never fought before!

If this, my father's sword, cleaves not man and horse,
I will break it o'er my thigh, though they cleave me worse;
Bring, bard, cross Channel, this rede to my hall:
"Thy master brought a hundred low before they made him fall!"

The Printed Grail

They came as clans would gather, the short, the lean, the fat,
For hunting of the wild book in its native habitat;
For two and thirty years they came, and who could say them nay?
And many storied treasures did they find and bear away.

When hours are slow and heavy then there grows a mighty need
When all is read beneath one's roof, and nothing left to read,
One voice will call the clarion, its echoes will be heard
To quench a thirst more terrible for an unseen printed word.

Stay not the tramp of many feet in search of their surcease,
Until they have their books in hand, a temporary peace;
The hair grows grey, the eyes grow dim, and still they haunt the
    shops
And only great Metraton knows the day their hunger stops.

The scholar starves—to save his life, he sells his dearest things
The worldly goods amassed in life by humble men and Kings;
But they have found a learned man, regardless of his age,
Has breathed his last with book in hand upon an open page.

The Inn at the Side of the Road

The sun in golden glory fades
At the end of a dying day,
And purple evening casts its shades
On those along the way.

The sunny hours they have toiled
'Mid orchard, field, and vine,
And now they trudge, with jerkin soiled,
To quaff their stoup of wine.

An amber glory, casked with love,
From cooling cellar depths,
The linkboys haul it up above
The ploughmen to refresh.

No vin sacre, from Abbé's hands,
May with these draughts compare;
The landlord well their thirst commands
As they his liquor share.

And well replete with tired feet
To home they turn away
To slumber till the morning greets
The men that cut the hay.

The Mask

What lurks behind the festive revel mask?
Some lady of a mystery profound;
Divining this were not a simple task,
But that which learned doctors might confound.
What hides behind this sparkling pair of eyes?
Some kalendar-prince, unknown to the crowd,
Or some yet undiscernible surprise
Whose secrets none may share, or voice aloud.
What hides behind the mask and roils the brain?
Is it a prelate from far Vezelay,
Or Prester John, come visiting again,
Replete with lore, and seeking gentler play?
Now tip the flagon, seek the noble flask,
And tipsy, we will peek behind the mask!

Yesudai

O little princeling, hearts have prayed for thee
From many lands, that thou may'st one day be
Their Shah, as were their old sires in their time,
And pledge thee hearts and hands right joyously.
Let this small object of our faith and love
No foolish words in praise need more to prove
Our service to thy House in gentler deeds
Than thy father hath, men's loyalties to move.
And when thy lady mother shews this poem
Mayhap the hand that wrote it will be gone,
But 'neath its breast, its heart prays victory,
God send thee better chamberlains than me.

The Honour of Princes

In the corner near the window of the ancient woodsmen's hut,
Chipped and cracked upon the sill there stood a crock,
And it armed itself in golden sunlight, and was happy, but
Its persistent thoughts began to chide and mock.

"When Duke William humbled Harold, draughts he drank from
silver ewer,
But the ceorl and cniht had only humble mugs,
No resplendent goblets might adorn the cupboards of the poor,
Save their earthenware and silent stony jugs.

"Yet in Stephen's time, when barons reived like wolves upon the
fold,
Sombre Desmoulins came limping on one leg,
And I do perceive he was not loath one groatsworth to lay hold
And drain my contents to the very dregs!

"And the elders of my village hearken back to olden time,
When the fathers of our Kings once kept their sheep;
Neither clothed were they in gold and purple; nothing so sublime,
Their fare was plain and they had time for sleep.

"And when Alfred needed fighters for his wedge to fight the Dane,
Women, priests, and linkboys then were soldiers all,
Ah! But now ex-Marshals are put to fearful pain,
And are not ranked with the fighters in their hall.

"'Tis the same with every Kingdom: when the Crown needs help to live,
Then it keeps its regulations short sand sweet,
And it lets them all contribute, who have anything to give,
But once they're out of danger, 'Vit! Vit! Vit!'

"So you serve your Kings in peril and from princes number friends,
And albeit you need never leave your wives,
You will find that they believe the means will justify their ends,
'In' with one King, 'out' the next for all your lives . . .

"I'd be happy in my exile if I knew my friends were safe
From the barnacles from whose necks hang the keys,
But my memories are fickle: now they lull and now they chafe,
And the sovereign's social clubs do as they please!

"We have learned, much to our sorrow, that few ever heed the truth,
And we all know realms are never saved by rhymes,
For the world seems fit for tyrants, for the lax and the uncouth,
But, please God, save our realm for better times!"

Moira

The mist arises over Tara's meads
And in the ebon vault of Heaven glow
A brilliant studded vault of diamond beads
Whose radiance illuminates below
That queenly dame, whose voice were loved by bards,
Who sings aloud the father of the stones,
And mendeth lives from former shattered shards,
And puts the flesh back on our whitened bones.
She leads to life us who had drunk despair
Down to its dregs, nor thought to live again,
Until her presence purified the air
On tree-girt, misty Stokes' ensorcelled plain.
Take, lady, these poor lines that almost live—
Would God I had the world and more to give!

They Also Rule, Who Only Stand and Baste

Down came the byrnie from the wall:
"The Saxon warriors must fall
Before Hardrada's swift attack—
And if they rally, beat them back!"
The shield-fire slept within its sheath,
The hounds came frisking underneath,
Whilst in the fjord, prows rose and fell
Abreast the tide's impatient swell.
The King's great cloak swirled as he turned—
His nose an aroma had discerned,
And while his huscarles chew their shields,
Into the buttery Harald steals,
And there in pannikin, sausage browns!
The King's face changes from a frown,
And as he packs the food away,
Turns to the cook: "My dear, I say—
What's England? 'Twill be there tomorrow—
To leave this joy would bring me sorrow!"
The Royal pleasure belches forth—
"To show you what your skill is worth,
When I own England, for my Queen,
Let Brekke reign—please pass the cream!"

The Ballad of the Four Sons

The House Le Jeune in Gaspardy
Four sons gave to its seigneury;
Robert, Charles, of epee and cloth
Despised cowardice and sloth;
The third, Rainulf, vow'd desire
To earn his own demesne entire,
Relinquishing his brother's bounty,
The richest noble in the country.
The baby, Hercule, man of iron,
Could strangle in his hands a lion.
Straightway after knightly tests
With spurs d'or clad before his guests,
He swore an oath to take the Cross
Ere Holy Sepulchre be lost,
And Rainulf, having heard the rede
Of puissance that the paynim breed,
Vow'd him as well he'd need no prod
To fight the good fight for his God.
(Betwixt his chess and his backgammon,
Betimes confused Jesu with Mammon.)
The second brother, apellez Charles,
Was balm to those fraternal quarrels
That broke the peace of Gaspardy

(Eke heads as well they broke, pardie!)
A frere of capitulary order,
Had lived in abbey near the border
Well-loved by those of De Jeune name,
Since no portion did he claim.
The eldest, Robert, his sire's label
Bore, confidently and able,
And Urban's messengers received,
Their tales he heard, and deeply grieved,
Yet he must stay and be maintained
By his vassals and vileins,
And ready aid and counsel give
The Crown, that his own honour live,
And ride to chase, and reckon tail—
A quiet life did him avail:
He was not parcel to the host
That Champagne's folk burnt to a toast,
Whilst Brother Charles would tell his beads,
And laymen shrive of their misdeeds.
The sound of vespers bells at dusk
To him was sweeter far than musk;
The Northmen long learned to evade
The House of God where De Jeune prayed,

For they might but his body hurt,
Whilst he in time would them convert.
'Twas doleful time for Odin's son
When that his day of rape were done.
Rainulf with his martial air
Took passage bound for Outremer
With Blaise de Confrevant and host
Whose plans agreed with his the most,
And 'Baby' Hercule silent hulked,
Honed his broadsword, sat and sulked,
Eager for the chevauchee
To quit him of this company.
In Syria they joined the ranks
Of Tancred's mob, with signal thanks
For Hercule seven pounds had lost
Over the side by tempest tost.
At Bat-al-Arslan they commenced
To earn their daily twenty pence.
The Order of the Southern Cross
Before that citadel was lost,
A heavy day for Christendom
When that sad rede was taken home.
Now this is how Hercule his name

Earned its everlasting fame.
With two swords in his hamlike fists
He smote as though he rode the Lists,
And paynim paladins went down
Well-hewed through from chops to crown.
Surrounded by the paynim horde
Was pierced, and went unto his Lord,
Whilst Rainulf loving not the fray,
Set spurs to horse and rode away,
For Tancred's needs were but a curse
To one who thought but of his purse.
When Louis rode from Antioch
With half his cavalcade in hock
Years later through El Quds' main gate,
Where gypsy beggars lay, and sate
A-begging alms of passersby
Beguiling them with faerie-lies,
His gaze fell on a tattered man
And carefully his mien scann'd.
'Twas Rainulf, Christ! And for his pains,
Gat beggary his ill-gotten gains:
At least Hercule died hero's death
And earn'd a rhyme in trouvere's breath.

And when the King sent home the word
To certify what he had heard,
A box containing beggar's bowl
Was all was left of Rainulf's soul,
For which Frere Charles then said a mass,
That his line came to such a pass.
And Robert, though confessible,
In mourning not accessible,
Doffed off his sable rainment for
A coat of verts with semee d'or,
And went from pews back to his mews—
The kind of life a Comte would choose!
Thus have we witnessed brothers four—
The noble, saintly, and traitor;
A brawny hero doomed to die
Beneath Philistia's burning sky.
What moral ye may take of this
Were not my judgment, this I wist;
Yet an this tale hath not amused
This company, my soul were bruis'd.
I pray Sire Dieux may hear my tune—
Take us to Heaven—but not too soon!

Aisling for Mary Radich

Two sisters dwelt in Royal Henry's time
Upon a grassy knoll nigh Cyladh Henge,
The elder, Aisling, long in Bardic rhyme
Sung far and wide, a name full far from strange.
The younger, Aravis, a child of Fire
Of spirits summoned from the bosky shaw,
A fay who kindled every heart's desire,
And saw with blue eyes more than mortals saw.
Aisling was courted by a gentle Knight,
Which same besmitten was of Aravis,
But lest they fade for aye each other's sight,
'Neath full Moon vanisht, whither, no one wist.
Alas! when hearts of fays love Adam's sons,
They must win all, else naught were truly won.

Sonnet LIII. R.E.H. Style #3

The overseers . . . how they smote and lashed,
How long they tried to kill all trace of me;
In Time's long night, when brazen armies clashed
Beneath the blood-red Moon of Tartary.
They chained me to a galley's lower deck
That plied the wine-dark seas of yesteryear;
Pale bones adorn the timbers of the wreck
To final rest had sunk whom others feared.
From every obelisk my name was rent;
In every humble hut, guest I was not
Excepting in the Midianite's distant tent,
Or leavening some myth of Camelot.
And even in this age, so hard to see,
Men die, their seed to dwell in liberty.

Quest

For we have digg'd and kept up late o' nyghts
Thro' shelfs of dustie tomes til mornyng lyght
And lerned mickel of forgottyn lore
That few who bokes reed hath lern'd bifore.
Who saith that oure quest were mayd in veyn?
For eftsoons sholde we browse these shelfs agayn
And wysdom geyn for our deliveraunce
Nor efort maik in more extravagaunce.
Who seekes these shelfs in derknesse fynds the waye
And maketh derkest nyght lyk unto daye.
Our guerdon haf we now that we haf seen
The oldest bokes that for yeares haf been
In shadowes cloked, bayrd unto our ken
And faine wolde we these shelfes serche ageyn.

Stand or Fall

I bore the wood to the forge and stood
Whilst sparks flew from the maul
That our smith near broke with a lightning-stroke
On the blade that was meant to fall
On what might stay to bar my way—
Daemon, god, or man,
When my Path was found on untrod ground,
Or on Them Outside who can,
As our Elders told while the blood ran cold
As of our vanished kith and kin
Who had lived one day but none could say
What fate they were meant to win.
And I carved the Signs in eldritch lines
Few human eyes had seen
On the gleaming blade our smith had made
For a task that had never been.
And today I lie 'neath a leaden sky,
With my broken blade in hand,
But my cold bride well served Those Outside
In a way men understand.

The Price of Blood

We marched out from Purutium in mail,
Our host the Epitymbia of old,
Although we knew it was to no avail
In summer, though our temperatures ran cold.
Between our gods and Others there was strife
That only by our swords' edge might be stayed,
And every man among us knew his life
Would rest upon the prowess of his blade.
'Neath Helios we trooped toward the fray
Without a rest and fearing we might lose,
Though through a Shadow covering the day
Our lives the only weapon we might use.
When finally we neared our unknown foe,
It was a Thing men were not meant to know.

Tiresias

Wrapt in the cloak of Nyx my sight still views
Through Monus transparent the truth of pain,
How time the Tree of Life steadfastly hews
Whilst cryptic presence succours it again.
Against the son of humans had we hope,
All else concealed beyond the veil of sight;
That hidden Outside where our vision gropes
And turns our hope of dawn to endless night.
My sage sire Cadmus of these had no ken,
Aegenor's son was but the child of Man;
From him I came into a world of Men
And never Beings known since Time began.
And though with triumph man may crown his strife,
In time the Darkness will reclaim his life.

Weighed in the Scales

Origin

In bower shaded from the glaring sun
We sought relief and waited for our breath
To voice our judgment, and we spoke as one—
The flagrant promise of elusive death.
No shadow stirred there as the hours crept
On silent tentacles that we discerned
Beyond our ken from aeons that had slept
That from our nascent consciousness had learned
Whence came the soul that fills this earthly form,
Bestowing on ourselves a hidden grace,
And sees those things that never had been born
In our familiar time and part of space,
And we still wonder what employs the skill
To vouchsafe life unto us by its will.

Ephemera

It brings the night on iridescent wings
Where sunset in its silent glamour waits
To mix a colour it will illustrate
The morrow that a gypsy current sings,
Where faded stars the inky skies await
From unbegotten origins their time
Remembering where they once ruled sublime
A firmament in luminous estate,
Departing with a dawn no eyes have seen
Where shadows linger, and their murky veil
On all things not apparent must entail
A memory of what has never been.
And from this dream it leaves upon the sand
A mark created by no human hand.

Chagrin

The world its venom hath, and more to spare
For spirits brighter than the common herd,
And spits a-plenty, poisoning the air,
Obscuring them who speak the gentlest word
And venom'd in its ichor, bleak and rude,
Must ever elevate its poorest part—
Who force the gifted to subside, and brood,
And falter, and corrupt the name of Art,
And thus 'twas ever: shew but gift of speech,
High quality of tone; demeanour soft,
But shew that ye can gentle mien teach,
And grudging hearts will bury thee as oft.
This Earth were shorn its hope of Heaven's meed
Though gracious spirits were its greatest need.

Sortilege

O Mars, in gaudy panoply display
Before more willing, sanguine protégés
Thy pretty toys, that older men refuse
To lay aside, but obdurately use,
And leave us to our scrolls and parchment sere,
To crumbling books and charmed atmosphere,
To chalices redolent with the fumes
Of incense from foul, stagnant Stygian tombs;
To worried glances from our fellow men,
To late-burned candles, parchment, ink, and pen,
To spells we dare not ever use again:
To retort, and to brazier well-supplied
With heated coals a-blazing white inside;
To ancient arts and dark philosophy
That illustrate arcane cosmologies;
To withered herbs, and Night's pale silver eye;
That softly lights the inky velvet sky;
And thus adorned is Nature's panoply
That earth seems all in perfect harmony:
So quiet one can hear an owl's grim heart
From whose fell swooping tiny creatures start;
And though the silence broods no swirling breeze,
We know not what sights, rustling through the trees;

And those of us who trim the flickering lamp
And greet Aurora with her mists and damp,
The smallest hours of the long night keep,
Remaining strangers to the thought of steep,
For daylight clamours and the haunts of men
Move not our mind, stir not our heart or pen;
The dreary rounds they keep for daily bread
As though an army of the living dead
No leisure knows wherewith to contemplate
The tides of Fortune, or the whims of Fate
That move them, unknown, to their Destiny,
The heavy silence of Eternity. . . .

A Fragrance

There is a fragrance on the vagrant wind
That hints of chartless seas and domed Cathay;
Suggests the golden pomp of ancient Hind,
And calls the dreamer from his dream away
To Oriental panoply and state;
To wharves piled high with spices from the East,
Where ancient seamen spin yarns of the fate
Of spectral sailors 'neath the sea, at feast,
Who plied the stormy seas, and could not rest,
And living, loved, and dying, earned renown,
Communing with the worst and with the best,
And laughed when Heaven hurled its lightnings down.
And we are made of dreams, who cannot be
More than a sigh in our own reverie.

Apathy

The palace of the Emperor at dusk
Is golden in the quiet setting sun;
The breezes from the garden bear their musk
To show the sweetness of the day is done;
'Neath carmeline engravings, in its tree,
The nightingale, with golden-throated song,
All hearts fills with its gentle reverie
That none need question, "Where do I belong?"
A tiny trickle from the fountain's heart
Fills seashell basins wrought of carven jade—
This is the place where miracles may start,
Where once the dainty Child of Heaven played.
Yet on their shaggy ponies near the wall,
The fur-clad riders wait the final call.

Futility

Khayyam was close from spirit deep within;
We build a vision of a Paradise
The selfsame Door we leave whence we came in—
And which man truly claimeth he were wise?
Wherefore gave Allah unto man a brain
That he his world might shape to his content,
When many must needs labour yet again
That Time be regained that was long since spent?
We stir the ashes of a long-dead blaze,
In which our youth was utterly consumed;
Instead of building now for better days,
In vain we hope lost years may be resumed.
We weep that we inherit such a state—
Man hath no wisdom—only God is great.

Damozel Alayne

Apollo's darts afflict the great and small;
In windrows doth he render nations prone;
The guard that paceth on the castle wall,
The aged cutler on his wheel of stone,
The fresh-faced, red-lipt maid with apple cheek,
The huddled crone amid her eldritch charms:
Thus each condition the Physician seeks
And every station and degree he harms.
Nor any Pope nor Emperor may flee
His lot in life, nor hope his weird to 'scape,
And therefore we thee counsel earnestly:
Do thou live life amid the merry grape!
We chivy thee: ne'er Sorrow take to wife,
But drain down to the dregs the Cup of Life . . .

Epitaph on an Unknown Howe in the Foothills of Wales

Repent, O man, thy Way shall not be long,
Nor is thy life forever given thee;
To this eternal earth dost thou belong,
Where all men sleep throughout eternity.
Behold this mossy bier in shady copse
That holds thy last remains as yet unknown;
The sunlight filters through the willow-tops
To trace its elfin patterns on thy stone.
So muse, therefore, and contemplate thine end—
Thou hast to this place followed worst and best;
The kindly earth must melancholy end
And thou at last may say "I am at rest."

The Poet to His Bed

O Bed, thou who, a caricature of Death
Dost measure us in sober, temporal breath,
Becoming, in those hours when we are ill,
A ship that sails beyond its captain's will;
Or when fatigued, the morn's wee hours grown late,
We sink, exhausted, on our couch of state,
And dream those dreams that fill the secret nooks
Our minds have wrought—these, not the stuff of books,
Have taught us our labour to complete
When we are well, our health and zeal replete,
Lest we lie, late o' nights, in sore torment,
And wrastle with dread phantoms overpent
And thus, O Bed, all things art thou to us:
In health or illness, thou, our omnibus
O'er vistas unseen by our mortal kin,
Gives us those sights that stay for them, unseen,
That, for the Righteous, seem their final spot—
But for the Wicked, such a different lot!

Angelique Perdue

A blade of grass, fresh-sprouted through the stone
Beneath a crypt below its lonely moon,
Is not so mournful as my heart alone,
Abandoned in a waste of deadly ruin
That breathes a solitude as still as death,
And thou apart! What elixir of proof
Hath temporal pow'r, restoring them to breath
Who lie, like me, 'neath carven stoned roof?
And fragile tendrils by pale moonlight kist
Enshroud with ivy memories these pains
That hold no hope, but looming through the mist
Dismays us with their melancholy strains,
A musick, icy echoes of the spheres
That keep time with the trickling of my tears . . .

Rendezvous

We dined with friends, and raised our glass in toast
And drank each other's health, and long we spoke
Of many things that we have loved the most,
And spoke in earnest, and could not evoke
A greater mirth—and when we said farewell,
We knew not when another day would fall
When we would dine again, and could not tell
When we would sit with comrades in that hall
In jest and earnest, with a snatch of song.
Sweet memories we made that would not fade,
And well I knew that it would linger long
And shield me at those times I am afraid,
And feel a sudden chill, a tenseness tight,
As we each made our way into the night.

Toilette d'Angelique

Let spikenard of Tarsos now abound
Like spring's first freshet, gentle as a lamb,
And Egypt's metopion flow around
Thy legs, which in this silver basin stand.
Crushed mint 'neath armpits; on eyebrows and eyes
The marjolaine of Koos from ewer tall,
And smoke of incense riseth to the skies
Through thy soft hair—a raven waterfall!
The Kyproian oinathe on thy heart,
Attar of roses on thy neck and cheeks;
Bakkaris on the dancer's hidden part,
The honey'd bastion wily Eros seeks,
And if we all these scents fix'd in one bowl,
They still fall short the sweetness of thy soul.

Meistersang

The Cherubim with gaudy streamers dip
Near verdant Terra's luxuriant meads;
Now proffers faun his vierge and nymph her lip
Whilst Mars and Phoebus dismount from their steeds,
And high Olympos' board is weighed with gold
Before which hopeful godlings ply their skill,
Each stanza new, yet in form, ages old,
And writ to do high Zeus' imperial will.
Now Peri pours the heady nectar out,
Yet each enchanting verse makes light the head,
Not knowing who will win this Bardic bout
And through tossed flowers to his crown be led.
How long must honest skalds their hour beg,
And know such rigmarole to lay an egg?

At the Inn

Full many miles I traveled down the Road
Till through the trees the sunlight dappled gold,
And hunger now became my driving mode
With fire's warmth for weary limbs and cold.
An ancient inn upon a crossroads stood,
Its high peaked roof a finger to the sky;
The landlord heaped the hearth with fresh-hewn wood
And shew'd to me the bed whereon I'd lie.
A wedge of Chilton and a pot of ale
And cheer he made in goodly fellowship;
He bade me, if I liked, to tell my tale
The while his company the brown ale sipp'd—
But ere I broached my word-cask he enquired
Wherefore go I bedight and so attired.

Samhain

The leaves are sere; a crimson carpet lies
On greensward, scattered by a restless wind
Aloft on Aeolus' breath from distant Hind
Beneath the louring grey October skies.
The primal Sacre de l'Autumne: to tread
Crisp ribbons underfoot, an annual rite
Until the sun, its glorious gilded light
A tenebrous curtain shrouds above its head.
Here omnipresent Shadow spreads its wings,
And things nocturnal float from misty ground,
The woods with wraiths uncanny here abound
And Nature mourns when earlier it sings.
Tread softly, sons of Man; the balance stays,
An equal measure to discern thy days.

A Peek at Dürer

In "Todentanz" the poet also reels:
He witnesses the great and humble move,
And knows what every other dancer feels—
These are the final steps of life and love.
Save for his rhyme, all striving is in vain,
In storied tower or in leafy glade;
It brings an end to every joy and pain.
Thus poets, like the rest of us, must fade.
They also dance, who by the dint of War,
Essayed to touch the Heavens with their spears;
They conquered or they fell—none could do more,
And now in vain are dropt their mourners' tears.
Dance on, while strength yet lingers in your frame,
For none of us will do this dance again.

Discovery

When Marquez set his foot upon the sand,
His hand upon the royal flag of Spain,
Not knowing what inhabited this land
Or what his quest was likely to attain,
The natives gasped a terrifying tale
Of something manifested from Outside
That made the Spaniards' countenances pale
And wish to find a refuge where to hide.
This was not what their Saviour could ward
Believers from an unheralded fate,
And every man with Marquez turned toward
Their longboat, lest before it was too late
They might depart the region and return
To Spain to warn about what they had learned.

Wrapped in Fabrics Red

Whoso will stumble on a dying world,
Its lofty towers ruins of its past,
Its avenues where pipers proudly skirled,
Their echoes swallowed up by Time at last?
Through bare streets the strange and dark One ranged,
No beasts to follow, no crowds to acclaim
His presence, nor consider him as strange,
Or fathom for what destiny he came.
And where long aeons dynasties held sway,
Their palaces had crumbled into dust;
Mad Chaos blew its particles away,
No steel, but only fragmentary rust.
Seek not for dying worlds, for they are gone,
And leave but phantoms to reflect upon.

Weighed in the Scales

Death is too proud—it claims both high and low,
Despite their hearts and deeds, their race or tongues;
The Keeper of the Gate through which all go
Receives the spirits of the old and young.
Howso we shift to hurry or to stroll,
Or whether we be craven men or brave,
The part of us that represents the soul
Is bound to rest at length beneath the grave.
How we the futile laurels strive to gain
Expending every effort since our birth,
Exerting strength, and taking every pain,
Our final destination is the earth
From whence we sprang, and thither are we bound—
The paths of fame end only in the ground.

To Clark Ashton Smith

Fear not—not come yet is thy final hour,
The rosy line of dawn is dormant still;
Enwrapt in gloom as petals of a flow'r
In patient silence lingering there still.
How deafeningly thy silent voice resounds,
Thy vision brighter than a thousand suns
Our corporal reality surrounds
As to the Infinite thy fancy runs.
Stay, Master; let us only touch thy robe,
And we of life's mirages shall be cured,
For farther vistas will our senses probe,
Not these insipid tales we have endured,
And we will seek and find where thou hast flown,
By Bards surrounded, never thee alone.

Conundrum

Wherefore did I seek? Tomes filled my shelves;
How hard it was the lure of books to pass
While other seekers satisfied themselves,
Still hypnotized by longing to amass
Those cryptic volumes offering that lore
The world had long ceased trying to obtain,
That rules the hours of sages who before
The Light of Learning started to explain
The mysteries of matter, time, and space.
The books I found were proven obsolete—
Millennia of learning were erased,
While all I gained were tired, aching feet,
And after seeking wisdom all in vain,
I left by that same Door through which I came.

Anomaly

In verdant oaken grove there stood a tree
Not laden with a rustling leafy crown
As were its sisters, showing loftily
Their green tiaras claiming just renown.
Its wizened limbs curled blacker than the night;
No songbird on its limbs with piping voice;
A single raven fluttering in flight
Its branches seeking refuge by its choice.
And here the corpse of Amos Krull had swung,
Left dangling till he rotted for his deeds,
And in no fireside ballad would be sung
Remembrance of his life for aught to heed.
A woody plant—yet sigil of the doom
The Erinyes had woven on their loom.

Raw, New Things

I am bound fast to many raw, new things,
Born in a city far from older lanes,
And grew with no one able to explain
The stranger feelings that the darkness brings.
I knew no treasure left from elder times,
With which a child in youth could be beguiled,
Nor tales of travelers to reconcile
Our ambience from a distant, foreign clime.
I had the daily round a child may know
Too willing to abandon with his youth,
And go to seek a darker, unknown truth
To where a child of restless spirit goes.
Those chains that hold me fast have not been filed,
For in my heart I still remain a child.

Phantasms

The Pathways of the Dead

Stay, stranger, for thou hast not ever been
Beyond the fields where men are wont to go,
Nor wrought what human eyes have never seen,
Nor know what sons of men should never know.
In places where the strong forbear to seek
Sleep things of darkness, lost to eyes of men,
That taunt the strong, and terrify the weak—
The Earth must never know their like again.
Thy mothers' sons for gentler deeds were born,
And not to labour, friendless and alone,
And never bound to stranger creeds outworn
That leads them to a destiny unknown.
Pray, turn from folly—when all has been said,
We will not seek the Pathways of the Dead.

The Lost Legend of Ingoldsby

After H. P. Lovecraft

Though why I need the Moon to skulk about
In lonely graveyard, while the haunts of men
Are filled with revellers who clink and shout
Oblivious to my Quest, while I again

Raise ancient lantern over weathered stone,
In hope of finding who by earth enclosed
Once laboured late of nights, though not alone
And wrought what Daemons to his mind disclosed.

"Essential salts," according to the Scroll
By which whatever lived may rise again
And breathe the Air of Life, as full and whole
As silent they had lain, forgotten men.

A moonless night had better cloaked my will,
Though it has never satisfied my needs,
And I will disappear behind the hill
And fools some day will guess about my deeds.

Justly cursed am I by Them Who come,
Through baleful shadows on this ground had crept
And this be now the tally and the sum
Of what I did, when that I might have slept.

A Lovecraftian's Eye-View of Kipling

When winter's chill effluxions cloud the air,
And night his cloak draws o'er the gabled peaks,
And church-spire turns to daemon-talon bare,
And elder folk their warmth and comfort seek,
Then I to Mr. KIPLING'S tome impel
My creaking footsteps on the parlour floor,
The frozen world of winter to dispel
With equatorial tales of Ranjipoor,
And this edition, but a hundred bound
Of fearsome things from Khyber's haunted pass
Regales my winter evening with the sound
Of tortured moanings from the Tartaric mass,
And yowling things from highest Himalay
Delight my appetite for the macabre
And move my sympathy from far away
With stifled groaning or with muffled sob;
Then I can sleep; thereafter I will sing
Of further joys tomorrow night will bring.

The Elder Ones

In cities and in hamlets there are homes
That unknown hands in olden times had reared
Of which we learned from dusty, ancient tomes
That stronger folk than we had rightly feared.
Grey shadows covered them in light of day
While deeper darkness gripped them in the night;
The elders of the town could never say
What made the passersby recoil in fright.
Bent trees that clustered round were dark and dry,
Nor on their limbs did songbirds build abodes;
An unseen cloud obscured the moonlit sky
And laid its shadow on their lonely roads.
What beings dwelt within no one can know,
They brood today as they did long ago.

The Lost City

We saw the city's turrets from afar,
Like dull-grey fruit above a crenelled wall;
Above its gate there hung a fiery star
And none gave answer to our hailing call.
Past winding ways of carven colonnades,
With daemon-faces leering at their crown,
We stealthily our cautious progress made,
But none of us had known a grimmer town.
Its terraces in unpropitious wise
Their dead trees lined a shapeless winding way,
And maps we lacked direction to devise
That might return us to the light of day.
O! stranger, turn thy feet from this travail,
And for thy soul's sake, find another trail.

The Book

We always wondered why he never showed
The book he told us he had hid away
From those who took the shadow-haunted road
To visit him, and none could ever say
Where he had found it, or what he had paid
To learn what it had hidden in its leaves;
And when to rest he finally was laid,
None who searched his bookshelves could conceive
Of where he had sequestered it, or why.
When visiting we had all feared to wait;
He learned the reason even Death might die
And leave our world in far more sorry state.
Some books resist, whenever they are read,
To teach their readers what their writers said.

Janandra

Independent of the seasons' flow,
You caught the light of learning in your trap,
And plot your journeys on a cosmic map
Where more mundane explorers never go.
And we, your crew, will not stop up your ears:
The Sirens' song falls silent as you close;
What charm is it that lures them from their tears,
That you have fixed from sunlight and from snows?
We wonder why the lion licks your hands,
Or why Dark Things assemble at your beck,
And why no scars appear upon your neck,
And why your mail arrives from unknown lands.
Your tales enthrall, and more than satisfy—
Your star shall one day rule the winter sky.

Predecessors

A more compelling voice than we had heard
Assailed our conscious presence in that tomb
Where deeper shadows than there had been room
Their wings spread like some predatory bird
As guardian sent, presiding at the Gate
Where stouter spirits in forbidden space
Let all know that an aeon-shrouded race
Had reared these structures, but refused to wait,
Their secrets by uncomprehending eyes
From vistas lost before the world was young,
Or lays in alien accents had been sung,
Their echoes quivering beneath the skies.
We rose to leave; before we turned around,
The Elder Sign glowed faintly on the ground.

Buried Truths

We ask ourselves the reasons that we drive
Our spades in places far from wonted ken
To unearth buried truths that other men
Had interred when their rulers were alive
In vaults where cryptic pictographic signs
On hidden, carven eidolons were reared
And in our presence showed what had been feared
When in the heavens baleful stars aligned
To prove that we were not the first to reign,
But elder Beings from a realm Outside
From which it was impossible to hide,
A sigil sent that They would come again
And over us resume their former sway
And blow the treasured dust of Earth away.

Caveat

A sibilant whisper breathed, "Thou must not see
The gate that opens to our thousand hells,
Where never rapture nor contentment dwells
And where in conscious state no one may be."
No restless wind its subtle digits probes;
None ken scant moments in which there is hoped
Elusive truths for which in vain are groped
And Nature is divested of her robes.
None may bear witness to this darkling void
Where never glimmered any hope of light
An anchorage where floats the Barque of Night,
And shadows of eternity have stood.
Return, then, from whence thou hast dared to go—
There are things man was never meant to know.

The Presence

Where daemons laughed, near noxious holes in space
In ages aeon-lost to questing minds
Before the advent of a sentient race,
There dwelt a Presence. There strange currents wind
And towers grim their spectral fingers showed
A gloomy sky, that by familiar strength
Were never reared as recognized abode,
So weird in height, uncanny in their length.
From them a tocsin chilled unwary hearts
Who saw horizons past their farthest rim
To where the edges of the cosmos starts—
The daemons' laughter gradually grows dim,
And, echoes dying, silently gives way
To Time's forbidden dawning of the day.

The Codex

Within figured walls of chalcedon,
Alive with daemons' glowing ruby eyes,
Upon an onyx altar set upon
A withered tome in baleful silence lies.
The crumbled yellowed leaves their secrets hold
From prying eyes in preterranean hand,
Impervious to heat or sullen cold
That none now living truly understand.
There spectres hover, pallid shadows all
Bound to ward by Powers long denied
Their antique state within this haunted hall
Where Time itself in mystic silence died.
This volume, doomed by Fate, may only be
A codex living eyes will never see.

Outpost

None knew if it had ever really been
A dwelling where the crone had made her home;
It felt for aeons that it had been seen
By late-night pilgrims wandering alone
Beneath a glowing spectre of a moon,
Lurking near a dark and derelict wood.
Beneath an ancient cauldron fagots hewn
A cheerless blaze on wizened kindling stood,
And it was rumoured there an essence lay,
Unknown too long to ordinary men,
A stranger to the influence of day,
Dark commerce with the hag it held, and when
Bleak figures from a Shadow near her door
A horrid glowing Sign malignant bore.

Somnambulist

The spires of metropolis are firm
E'en swathed at midnight in a misty cloud,
Nor need the errant passerby to squirm
Lest phantoms imperceptible enshroud
His passing form with insalubrious light—
Here tales have wandered off on ancient ways;
No lingering rumour waiting to affright
Our citizens in these enlightened days.
The distant echo of an auto's horn
Dispels the vision hovering nearby
And soon the rosy fingers of the dawn
Draws Nyx her dark veil from Aurora's sky;
Yet whither human habitations be
There dreams a lingering hint of mystery.

Witness

No twilight masks the gloom of brooding hours
That creep on tiptoe, silent as the night
Divested of the slightest shroud of light
Left by things Outside by their cryptic powers.
At hours like these half-shuttered windows cast
Pale lamplight weakly lighting empty streets
Where isolated specters almost meet
Until the dawn dislodges them at last.
For this is when few bards recall the spores
That grow in Sarnoth and abandoned lands
By seas engulfed where towers used to stand
And waters drowned from sight primordial shores,
And none behold now what the stars disclose
To any save the One who truly knows.

A Lovecraftian Reads Caesar Midnight on Hallowe'en

Thinkst thou that so dark a ruin lies
On our insensate spirits when we sleep?
These portents for our weal bestride the skies.
And flown those angels that are wont to keep
Whole Man's estate, come what alarums may—
A lion in the streets that voids our eye,
Or Bird of Night that wisdom in affright
Our waking hours like unto Death decry
Our safety like unto babes i'the night;
Here cometh the Opener of the Way
Twixt earthly realm and none who live hath sight
And Them to Who Come whom none durst say nay.
Great Caesar duly bendeth to their will,
And in our souls their echoes hover still.

Silent Watchers

Seek no more—we are the Walkers Between,
Of subtle shade and doubt less than Man's ken
Who bide where worldly things are scarcely seen
And once discerned, are seldom known again.
A fortress from your labours you have made
While at your elbow, unseen by your eye
We who your dimension may invade
A greying force betwixt the Earth and sky.
Do not therefore deny that from the first,
Before Man's shadow fell upon the Earth,
We came to slake an unalterable thirst
Whilst none of your race felt what Man was worth.
We linger yet, abiding by your side—
Seek no escape—there is no place to hide!

The Shop

A store there was my friend had found alone
On Thirteenth Street one dark November day
Where books distracted those chilled to the bone,
Some borne at length from places far away.
A few tomes hoary with an age unguessed;
Decrepit covers, pages left unbound.
He paid for one a pittance, and the rest
He left abandoned, where they had been found.
Once again to Thirteenth Street he came
The next year when the air was bright with spring,
But at that address nothing was the same;
A boutique stood—a curious, puzzling thing,
That made him wonder what if he had seen
The single book that never should have been.

The Steeple

I listened long, but no saturnine tones
From this forbidden steeple ever came,
Its weathered churchyard said to hold the bones
Of certain people of peculiar name.
Late passersby walked at increased pace
When clouds obscured the moonlight from the street;
The townfolk were perturbed so near this place
And fearful of what they might chance to meet.
It brooded over ancient cobbled ways
With gabled houses from a time unknown,
Erected during long-forgotten days
The town but scarcely reckoned as its own,
And when the sun had set, the steeple dreamed
If things that had not been what they had seemed.

Recompense

None in our hamlet ever knew her age,
But when she passed we felt a sudden chill,
And few would seek a reason to engage
To hear her prattle of their own free will.
The sable feline on her window-ledge
Was known to be more than a household pet;
Exotic herbs next to her garden hedge
Long flourished and continue growing yet.
Her omnipresent garment was the hour
When moonlight bathed the churchyard in its glow,
Nor any guess was made about the pow'r
That she was thought to exercise as though
In service to the dark and evil lord
For some unfit ambiguous reward.

Chiaroscuro

Upon this cryptogenic web were Signs
In aeon-shrouded times when Beings wove
With strands from far-flung realms its obscure lines
That time and matter had no force to move.
Vague shadows reached for distances unknown.
An immanence of unfamiliar state,
The here and now as has been clearly shown
Bear fruit more suitable to contemplate.
From this far-distant Pharos blends a light
With sombre shades entwined no eye may mark,
That glows beyond the ordinary sight
And translates day into eternal dark.
This web is only manifest to him
Who can see all, yet things like these are dim.

Impasse

Blood speckled bright the lonely snow-clad hill
In the gloaming of a boreal fall
Where it had appeared to drink its fill
Remote from hovel, hamlet, or from hall.
On Oceanus' western bank where dwelt
A race long vanished in the aeons past
Before the snowbanks had begun to melt,
A youth with thews of iron at the last
Barred its way and pierced it with a sword
With silver plated. There it could not pass,
That stream, for older law than cryptic word
Ruled daemons of this sepulchral class.
No humans live where prospered once this race,
Nor has such daemon ever shown his face.

Volte-Face

I have seen Yuggoth farther than the Rim,
And truly hope to never see again
That Thing entomb'd, for it was surely Him
Who came from Outside to the world of men.
I burn the tomes of Elder Lore, and fly
In fear that burns the centre of my soul,
Nor ever seek to sit and ponder why
This quest has left my substance less than whole.
No more do crumbling volumes catch my eye,
Nor do their mysteries compel my heed,
For in forbidden books their silent cry
Were more than any seeking heart could need.
Apage! I have put myself beyond
That for which other seekers seem so fond.

The Sword

The Dark Barbarian towers o'er
Proud cities reared by men,
Yet he would learn one lesson more
Held I my sword again.

From fallen star its metal
Was forged by ancient hands,
Old smiths of cryptic fettle
Who fared from unknown lands.

Ere R'lyeh sank, before the Sun
Rose o'er the spires of Mu,
Their hammers had their work begun
As only they could do.

An edge it bore, none near as keen
A film of silk could cleave;
More potent stroke was never seen
That gods could scarce conceive.

And if I bare this brand again
Let reivers bring their horde,
And they will learn what kind of men
Deserve to wield my sword!

Pale Visitor

How he found me, I shall never know,
Old Bones in shadowed hood with ember eyes
Sat at my table and began to throw
With grimace his uncanny set of dies.
I shrugged and drew a chair before his face,
For he was never servitor of Fate,
Or sworn antagonist, although our race
Knew not his will until it was too late.
I cast his dice and scored a final throw;
My guest not once concealed his wonted grin,
A wise expression all of us should know
This game impossible for us to win,
And when he left, a scorch-mark on his chair
Remained the only sign he had been there.

The House

The secret of the house was kept concealed
For countless ages when the line expired
According as its family desired
Secure in silence as had been revealed.
When strangers came and purchased the estate,
Their aspect had a rare and alien mien
Much unlike any who were ever seen
And few approached to linger at the gate.
No light was shown on any moonless eve;
A single greying servant rarely seen
When asked refused to detail what had been
The reason few had let themselves believe
The house had ever been a rightful place
Of any of a more familiar race.

The Street

It came as though a vertiginous dream
That Morpheus had spited my repose—
The vision of a cobbled street that teemed
With loathsome creatures no sound person knows.
On either side decaying dwellings loomed,
Their shadows falling darker than the night;
They made me feel as though I would be doomed
To lose the sanctuary of the light.
A bitter chanting quavered in my ear
And wafted into every cryptic hole;
It gripped me with a frightful nameless fear
And trapped the very essence of my soul.
And when I woke, some time it was until
My trembling ceased, and I again was still.

Wyckham

When English feet first trod this rocky soil
Upon this windswept coast hard by the sea,
They searched for places to reward their toil,
Unwarned of Presences they could not see.
The natives' omens caused but slight concern,
And more than once they wandered carelessly
On dark hills where such baleful fires did burn
And muffled echoes rose continuously.
The remnant of their log-reared chapel stood,
Its cobwebbed portal open to the storm
Hard by a lonely, shadow-haunted wood
Where eerie things concealed their cryptic form;
And to this day all strangers have been told
The reason that this land was never sold.

Phantasm

No one has seen the visions I have seen
From early youth until the present day,
In nature or the dwelling where I lay
Fell Beings from Outside where none had been.
In blood-red sunsets shades of greying tone,
The eerie nightmares of a fearful waste
That lowered but did not recede in haste,
Have left me feelings few have ever known.
On bleak deserted streets lurked bestial forms;
Weird towers cast their shadows on the street
That never had been laid for human feet,
But phantom creatures of the night and storm.
These were my legacy, and few remain
Of things I hope I never see again.

Erato

O, sister, whence art thou unto us come?
Our road with peril fraught and none to guide
Hath reached since youth until our strength were done,
And shelter there was none wherein to hide.
From Bekra, long timeworn when Khem was old,
The mystic lyre did bear thee as our Sign,
Thou, who ancient tales as yet untold
Whose Singers served as Luna-masters' kine.
Upon our hearts thine ancient Seal was set
That binds us to some covert Being still
For aeons till our Destiny were met
And we our geas may finally fulfill;
And when their tattered banners they unfurl,
They will again reoccupy the world.

The Wanderer

Who knows where he had gone when he departed?
To unknown lands removed from human ken,
Or to the origin whence he had started,
So evanescent to the grasp of men?
Through troubled dreams we sought to catch a glimpse
Of where his footsteps led to distant ends,
His way by foemen hindered, or by imps
Abroad through wills a cryptic daemon sends;
And long those whom he left behind lamented
With all their tears and orisons in vain;
No explanation of his fate presented
Nor any sign he would return again,
Save one small token—this was all he left,
Where Time and Space displayed their single weft.

The Donjon

Upon an oaken table black with age
The wizened fingers turned a yellowed page
And sunken eyes examined hoary script
That from the grasp of daemons had been ript.
No human eye had seen what had been writ
For aeons lost, for Mages only fit,
To ken lost lores in covert chambers hid,
Obeying secret laws as they were bid.
With violet glow a single candle glowed,
Revealing to what hideous sources owed
This lone archaic Dweller in the Dark
Who with a tattered riband made a mark
The whilst the candle flared and shadows threw
Against the stony paling that so few
For centuries forgotten ever saw
According to an ancient banished law.
This darkened donjon, kept from human sight,
Had witnessed things that dwelt not in the light
And thither undimensioned worlds were known
That for long ages slept beneath these stones,
In twilight stage, awaiting but the Signs
That had been wrought in terrible designs
Illegible to anyone save who

Their dread and cryptic message surely knew.
The keep wherein this hidden chamber stood
Was never credited with any good,
And passersby would cross themselves and speed
Their pace to quit themselves with desperate need.
It stands today, a bleak and empty place
In which few men have ever shown their face.

Rubaiyat of Rub al-Khali

In our drear waste no thousand blossoms grown
Nor twist the desert and what has been sown
    Can any see a Sign gleam in the Sky,
For all that Man knows is forever flown.

Hither cacodaemons show no form,
Nor boast the aethery garments they have worn,
    Beguiling all the vision men have seen
Between Creation and the Final Morn.

Here in this crumbling caravanserai
For centuries where weary the Hadji lie
    And where the strange dark One was thought to bide
And whom the fellahs owned a mystery.

And in the scroll-house lieth yet that Tome
Long accursed from whither it had come
    That plagued for aye whoso its leaves dared turn
And rendered unto them an unknown doom.

And when the voice of Ubbo-Sathla rings,
Naught green from this forgotten wasteland springs,
    But echoes only of the fear that lurks
Behind each dune to which His shadow clings.

The servants of the Prophet warn the man
Who bideth hither, since the world began,
        For what he seeketh hath not ever been
By any mortal vision ever seen.

And when ye reach the leaf whereon was writ
By hand long gone that bade all use their wit
        And close the tome, and pass along thy Way
Nor read a single further line of it.

The Journey

By One by Whom this universe were made
I found at last at threescore years and ten
Myself abandoned where no man had stayed

Off on a Path that wound far from the Way
That in the past pursued by other men
Who passed but in no other wise could stay.

In murky forest where I fared alone
And saw such marvels few could now believe
Nor hoped to see ere that my life were done,

It felt as though those Outside hovered nigh
Of what strange shape or form no man could ken
And moved with dread intent through earth and sky.

No ring I conjured as the ancients wrought
For nameless things were wont to be evoked
To banish which no sage were ever taught.

As though in fearful dream I saw their shades
Bizarre in aspect, never sprung from earth,
And knew not whence our world did they invade.

For in a lifetime many things are known
That human mind had never thought could be
And man had liefer never claim his own.

Such beings in Fancy's net had ne'er been caught
In ancient mythic tales alone to be
But in man's reason never had been thought.

Tall bordering oaks rose stately by the Way
As crisp leaves trod unknowing underfoot
And frightened, neither slowed nor stopped to pray

Where neither sun nor darkness bathed the trees
More ancient than the memory of man;
Strange were the scents I inhaled on the breeze.

Although unknowing of the way to go,
What cryptic things might lurk upon my Path
I knew not what but still I wished to know!

For shapes not human cast behind my Road
Horrors never fit for human ken,
Like seeds of Cadmus by Yog-Sothoth sowed.

I wished that I had gone another way,
Amazed as I be after these events
That I survived unto the present day.

Off the Beaten Track

They were not "woods" in the normal sense—
Trees are not often feared,
And Nature gives us recompense
Quite seldom acting weird.
I had been this way a hundred times,
But to my great surprise,
I felt the oaks and stately pines
As though they had grown eyes.
The deeper in I found my way,
The darker it became,
The woods I walked through on that day
Were somehow not the same.
I never thought a wood-grown track
Was anything to dread,
But I could feel behind my back
Eyes bore into my head.
I asked what unknown things are there
This forest had not known?
I felt a chill upon the air,
No longer felt alone.
At last I found a lonely road
And left the trees behind,
A strangely dim and dark abode
Of unfamiliar kind.

The Pit

It had been little more than just a pit
That workmen left on the farm of a friend
In Pennsylvania when we witnessed it
The first time after letters that he'd send
Requesting us to set aside some time
To come and see his labours in the soil;
The pit was dry, its sides uncaked with slime,
In no way the result of his own toil.
But underneath the moon the pit became
Something much more than just a hollowed ground,
And an aspect overtook the terrain
That made it different from what we had found.
One felt as though more than a modern spade
Had scooped away the rocky, grainy earth
And started excavating and had made
More than a half-hour's digging had been worth.
Today, mist-shrouded, open to the sky,
It lies in silence, no one asking why.

The Keep

A sanctuary, lost in far Aran,
Its aether overborne with mystery—
No clue apparent of its history—
Loomed in a lonely place devoid of man;
And from its tower, older than the stone
That held it isolated in the breeze
Whose icy fingers probed within its trees,
No human ear had heard its eerie moan.
None knew or dared make question of its source;
No mark appeared on any noted chart;
Of those who felt its presence from the start,
No living being shewed for it remorse.
None ever its elusive tale would trace,
The sure sign of an enigmatic race.

The Travelers

For years we used their airways to escape
The putative ennui that I was told
Had us in its ineluctable fold
As mummies were in Khem's long-faded tape.
To stranger lands than home to which we flew
Where secrets had for aeons lain untold
And travel saw the both of us grow old,
Not knowing what the endless ages knew.
In every land and clime lay those Outside
And whence they came no human ever told
And less wise than those who had been bold
From whom it folly was to try and hide,
And to this day to distant places fly,
This destiny bequeathed us till we die.

Breinigsville, PA USA
04 January 2011
252640BV00003B/14/P

9 780984 480265